W9-BFG-181

Life in the World's Biomes

Ocean Plants

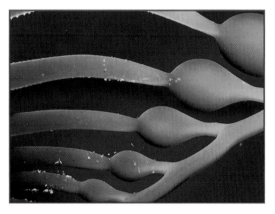

by Pamela Dell

Consultant:
Ian A. Ramjohn, PhD
Department of Botany and Microbiology
University of Oklahoma
Norman, Oklahoma

Capstone
press

Mankato, Minnesota

Bridgestone Books are published by Capstone Press,
151 Good Counsel Drive, P.O. Box 669, Mankato, Minnesota 56002.
www.capstonepress.com

Library of Congress Cataloging-in-Publication Data
Dell, Pamela.
    Ocean plants / by Pamela Dell.
    p. cm.—(Bridgestone Books. Life in the world's biomes)
    Summary: "Tells about a variety of ocean plants, how they are used, why they are in danger, and
how they are being protected"—Provided by publisher.
    Includes bibliographical references and index.
    ISBN 0-7368-4322-1 (hardcover)
    1. Marine plants—Juvenile literature. I. Title. II. Series: Life in the world's biomes.
QK103.D45 2006
579'.177—dc22   2004029140

Editorial Credits
Amber Bannerman, editor; Jennifer Bergstrom, designer; Kelly Garvin, photo researcher;
    Scott Thoms, photo editor

Photo Credits
Bruce Coleman Inc./Debra P. Hershkowitz, 16; M. Timothy O'Keefe, 6 (left); Ronald L. Sefton,
    6 (bottom right)
Corbis/Ralph A. Clevenger, 4
Corel, 1
Getty Images Inc./National Geographic/Michael Lewis, 14
Marty Snyderman, 8, 10
Minden Pictures/Flip Nicklin, cover
Nature Picture Library/Martin Dohrn, 20
Seapics.com/Doug Perrine, 12
Visuals Unlimited/Richard Herrmann, 18; Wim van Egmond, 6 (top right)

The author thanks Dr. Judith L. Connor, Director of Information and Technology Dissemination at Monterey Bay
Aquarium Research Institute, in Moss Landing, CA, for her generous and valuable input about the amazing world of
ocean plants.

1 2 3 4 5 6 10 09 08 07 06 05

Table of Contents

Oceans

From out in space, the earth looks like a big blue marble. The earth looks this way because oceans cover most of it.

Beneath the surface of the ocean lies a world of plants. These plants need sunlight, just as plants on land do. Ocean plants live where the sun shines on them. Plants grow in all but the deepest, darkest areas of oceans.

◀ Underwater plants, such as kelp, need sunlight to grow.
Giant kelp can grow up to 200 feet (61 meters) long.

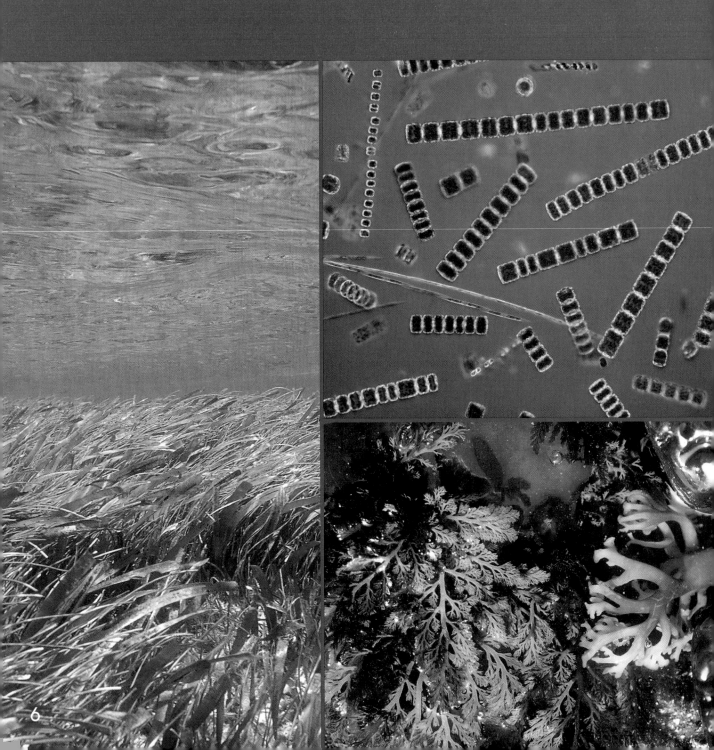

Ocean Plants

Some ocean plants live in shallow water near land. Nori, a red seaweed, clings to rocks. Sea grasses, such as turtle grass, grow on the ocean floor. These plants stay in one place.

Other plants drift with ocean **currents**. Tiny plants called **phytoplankton** stay near the surface of the water. They often gather in bunches.

◄ Turtle grass (left), phytoplankton called diatoms (top right), and seaweed (bottom right) all live in oceans.

Ocean Plant Features

Ocean plants have ways to hold their ground. Seaweeds and sea grasses have holdfasts. Holdfasts are root-like growths. They keep plants hooked to rocks or to the ocean floor.

Most freshwater plants would die in salt water. Ocean plants such as seaweed use salt water. Mangroves **filter** salt water. They flush out the salt to get the freshwater they need to live.

◄ Holdfasts help keep kelp from floating away.

Plant Homes for Animals

Sea grass meadows are homes to all kinds of creatures. Small fish, sponges, and sea urchins live there. Eelgrass meadows are like busy underwater cities. Eelgrass is home to more animals than almost any other ocean plant.

Ocean plants also make good hiding places for animals. Underwater, crabs scamper among the giant, waving stalks of a kelp forest. They hide in this brown seaweed. Eels and fish also rest there.

◄ Most rays live on the ocean floor. This bat ray swims through an eelgrass bed.

Food for Animals

Sea grass is an important food for ocean animals. Manatees, crabs, and young fish eat sea grass.

An important link in the ocean food chain is phytoplankton. Small fish eat phytoplankton. Large fish eat small fish. This **cycle** is a food chain. Without phytoplankton, small fish might starve. Then, large fish would have nothing to eat.

◀ Manatees can eat more than 100 pounds (45 kilograms) of plants in one day.

Plants Used by People

Seaweed is an important food for people in many parts of the world. Seaweed is a good source of vitamins and minerals. Many people eat rice, fish, or meat wrapped in seaweed. Cooks sometimes add seaweed to soups and sauces. Seaweed is often added to ice cream and yogurt. It makes these foods smooth and creamy.

Seaweed is also added to other things to make them thick. Sometimes seaweed is added to soap and paint. It is also used in toothpaste and hand cream.

◀ Workers plant seaweed in rows in the Indian Ocean. Later, the seaweed is picked, sold, and used in many products.

Plants in Danger

People are the biggest danger to ocean plants. People throw millions of gallons of waste into oceans every day. Garbage and chemicals **pollute** oceans. Pollution kills ocean plants.

Fertilizers also put some plants in danger. People put fertilizers on their lawns. When lawns are watered, fertilizers seep through the soil. Fertilizers then flow into rivers and oceans. These fertilizers help weedy ocean plants grow. Weedy plants take light away from other plants in the ocean.

◄ Garbage and other pollution kills ocean plants.

Protecting Ocean Plants

People all over the world are working to protect ocean life. Some countries have passed laws to lessen pollution. On land around the Gulf of Mexico, programs that limit fertilizer use have begun.

People can write to lawmakers about protecting ocean plants. People can support laws that help oceans. Oceans cover most of the earth's surface. Clean oceans keep the earth healthy.

◄ Scientists take samples of eelgrass beds to make sure they are healthy.

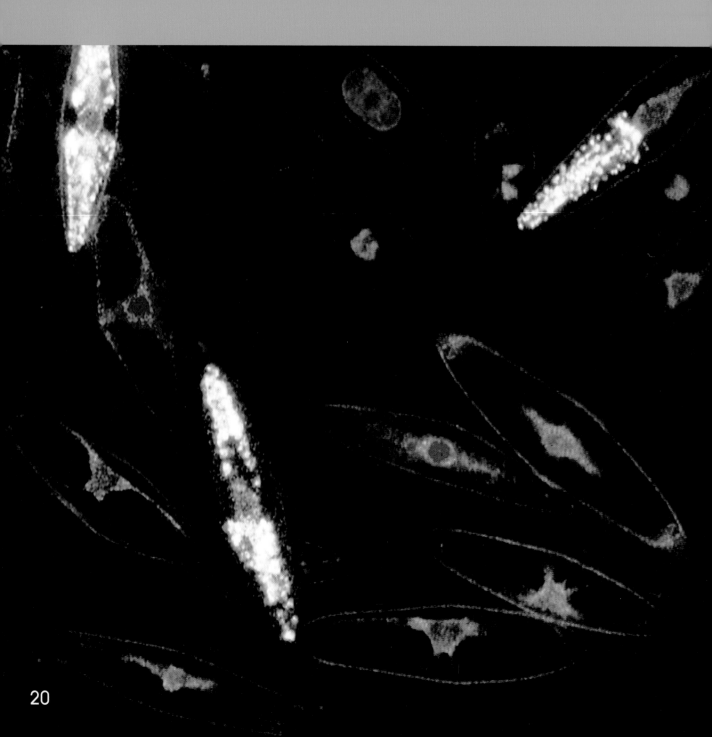

Amazing Dinoflagellates

Dinoflagellates (dye-nuh-FLAH-jel-uhts) are tiny, but amazing, ocean plants. Dinoflagellates are a type of phytoplankton. They come in many shapes.

Some dinoflagellates produce their own light. After a sunny day, the nighttime ocean sometimes sparkles like diamonds. This glittering light comes from millions of dinoflagellates floating in the water.

◀ Dinoflagellates glow at night.

Glossary

current (KUR-uhnt)—the movement of water in the ocean

cycle (SYE-kuhl)—something that happens over and over again

fertilizer (FUR-tuh-lize-ur)—something added to soil to grow larger plants; some fertilizers can hurt ocean plants and animals.

filter (FIL-tur)—to clean water; when mangroves and salt grasses filter salt water, they take out the salt.

phytoplankton (FITE-oh-plangk-tuhn)—tiny plants that drift in oceans; phytoplankton are too small to be seen without a microscope.

pollute (puh-LOOT)—to make dirty; garbage and chemicals pollute air, water, and soil.

Read More

Baker, Lucy. *Life in the Oceans.* World Book Ecology. Chicago: World Book, 2001.

Richardson, Adele. *Oceans.* The Bridgestone Science Library. Mankato, Minn.: Bridgestone Books, 2001.

Internet Sites

FactHound offers a safe, fun way to find Internet sites related to this book. All of the sites on FactHound have been researched by our staff.

Here's how:
1. Visit *www.facthound.com*
2. Type in this special code **0736843221** for age-appropriate sites. Or enter a search word related to this book for a more general search.
3. Click on the **Fetch It** button.

FactHound will fetch the best sites for you!

Index